Amazing Science Discoveries

BIOLOGY

The story of the animal kingdom

Dr. Bryson Gore

Aladdin / Watts

London • Sydney

CONTENTS

© Aladdin Books Ltd 2009

Designed and produced by Aladdin Books Ltd
PO Box 53987
London SW15 2SF

ISBN 978 0 7496 8647 5

First published in 2009
by Franklin Watts
338 Euston Road
London NW1 3BH

Franklin Watts Australia
Level 17/207 Kent Street
Sydney NSW 2000

Franklin Watts is a division of Hachette Children's
Books, an Hachette Livre UK company.
www.hachettelivre.co.uk

A CIP record for this book is available from the
British Library

Dewey Classification: 570

Printed in Malaysia

Editors: Katie Harker, Vivian Foster
Design: Flick, Book Design and Graphics
Illustrators: Q2A Creative
Picture research: Brian Hunter Smart

The author, Dr. Bryson Gore, is a freelance lecturer
and science demonstrator, working with the Royal
Institution and other science centres in the UK.

Introduction

Humans have practised BIOLOGY – the study of all living things – for hundreds of thousands of years.

In what ways are we the same as other animals, and in what ways are we different? How did the species we see on Earth today come into being?

People have always looked for an explanation as to how all the different life forms came into being.

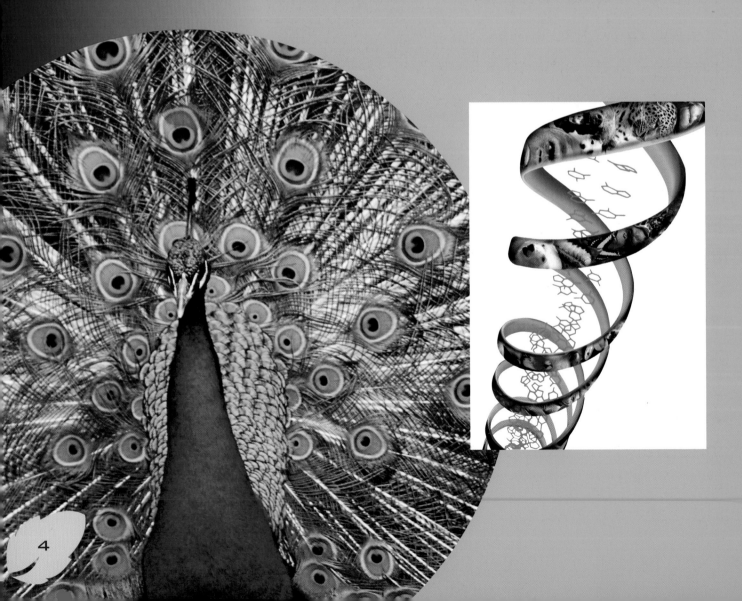

Now, many people believe it to be through evolution.

As scientists started to look at the age of the Earth, they realised that life had existed on our planet for millions of years. Fossil records show how these species have changed.

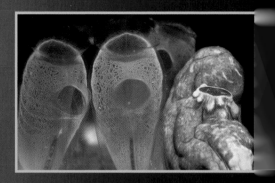

Animals have learned to adapt over the years to changes in climate. Some have learned to live in hot places, while others are able to withstand extreme cold. But the world is now changing at such a fast rate, we don't know whether these animal species will be able to adapt. Are we about to see many of the animals we know become extinct?

This book looks at twelve of the most amazing biological discoveries. Find out more about famous scientists like Darwin and Mendel. Learn how they used their skills to make sense of species and their genetic code.

Using the fact boxes will help you understand more about the world of animals. Learn about the amazing skills and feats of the animal kingdom.

How do we know?

Some great scientists opened our eyes to how evolution has developed all the species of animals that we see today. Gregor Mendel, an Austrian monk, studied pea plants and realised that they were passing on information about themselves in a form of code. This is referred to as a 'genetic code'.

All living things use DNA to pass on their genetic code. DNA is a very long spiral molecule that controls how cells behave.

English scientist Charles Darwin studied living things on his travels. He found that animals of one species stay similar to each other as they breed, and can adapt to change.

ALL ANIMALS ARE DESCENDED FROM A SINGLE SPECIES

The Earth today is home to billions of different species of animals, plants and bacteria. Scientists now believe that every living creature comes from a single species that lived million of years ago.

The science of . . .

Humans are an example of a single species of animals – just like cats and cobras.

Where did all these different animals come from and what makes them different? Fossils (*right*) reveal the history of life.

Scientists believe all animals evolved from a single, worm-like species that lived around 700 million years ago. It is thought their offspring evolved into every species of animal alive today.

ALL MAMMALS LIVE FOR ABOUT ONE BILLION HEARTBEATS

Mammals make up a single group of animal species and have many things in common. Scientists now know that mammals live for almost exactly the same number of heartbeats.

How do we know?

All mammals feed milk to their young. The milk is produced in mammary glands, which only mammals have. Mammals are 'warm-blooded', which means they need extra food and a nice fur coat to keep out the cold. Other species use scales (e.g. reptiles) or feathers (e.g. birds).

All mammals have exactly the same number of bones. Did you know that a giraffe has the same number of bones in its long neck as a human or a mouse?

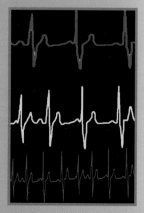

Mammals have hearts that pump blood into their lungs and around their bodies. The heart of a mouse is thousands of times smaller than that of a whale, but apart from size they are almost identical.

Heartbeats are recorded by ECGs (Electrocardiograms)

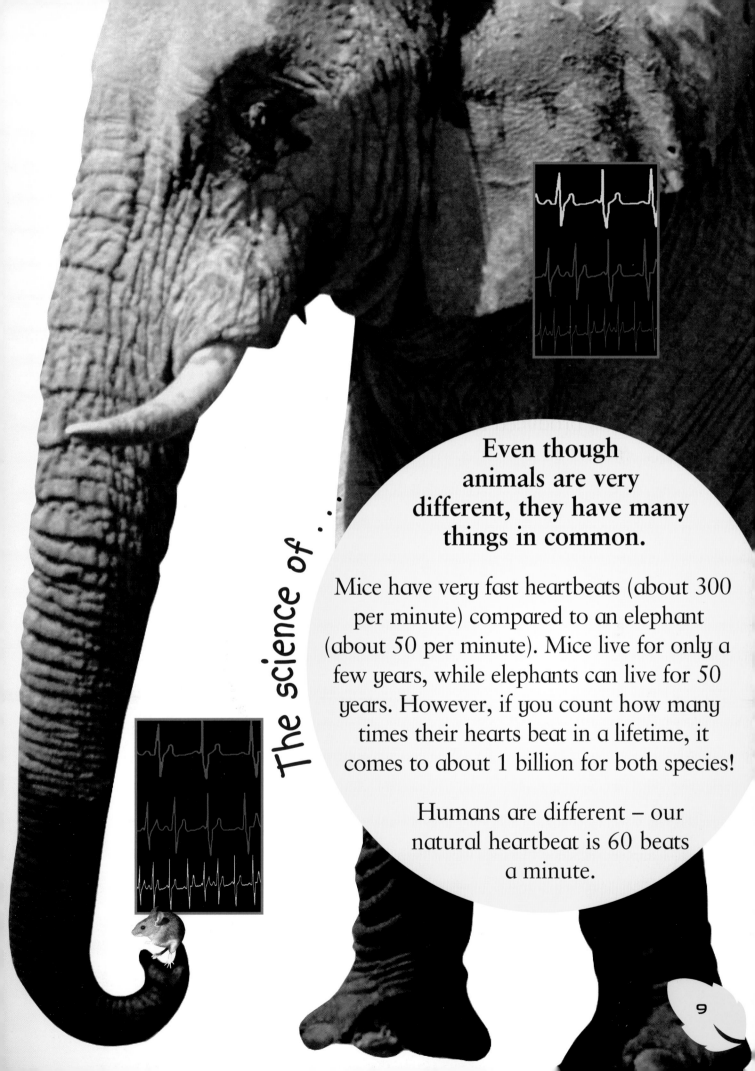

The science of ...

Even though animals are very different, they have many things in common.

Mice have very fast heartbeats (about 300 per minute) compared to an elephant (about 50 per minute). Mice live for only a few years, while elephants can live for 50 years. However, if you count how many times their hearts beat in a lifetime, it comes to about 1 billion for both species!

Humans are different – our natural heartbeat is 60 beats a minute.

SPIDER SILK IS STRONGER THAN STEEL

Humans have developed some of the most sophisticated materials in the world – steel for skyscrapers, Kevlar for stopping bullets and drugs to cure illnesses. But these are nothing compared to nature's own substances.

The science of...

Spiders make different types of silk for different purposes.

They use a sticky silk to catch their food. They use a strong silk as a 'safety line', and for the 'spokes' of their web. We know this silk is stronger than steel!

The cuttlefish (*right*) only has one bone, but it is a very special bone. It is made up of millions of boxes, each less than 1 millimetre across. To keep it afloat, the cuttlefish fills each box with gas, the same way a submarine uses air.

How do we know?

The animal kingdom produces materials for its own needs. We have learnt how to adapt these materials for our own use.

Silk is one of these natural materials. It is farmed on a massive scale with over 100,000 tonnes of silk produced each year. It is made from the cocoons of silk worm caterpillars. Each cocoon is made from a single fibre that can be over 1 kilometre long.

Experiments have shown that spider silk is stronger than steel. For this reason, scientists attempted to farm spider silk for commercial use. This was difficult because the spiders did not like being crowded together and tended to fight. So scientists tried transferring the DNA for spider silk into the genetic code for goats. Goats can now produce spider silk in their milk.

An ant can lift 50 times its own weight

Could you lift yourself off the ground? Do you think you could lift two friends up at the same time? Ants and fleas can. How do they do it?

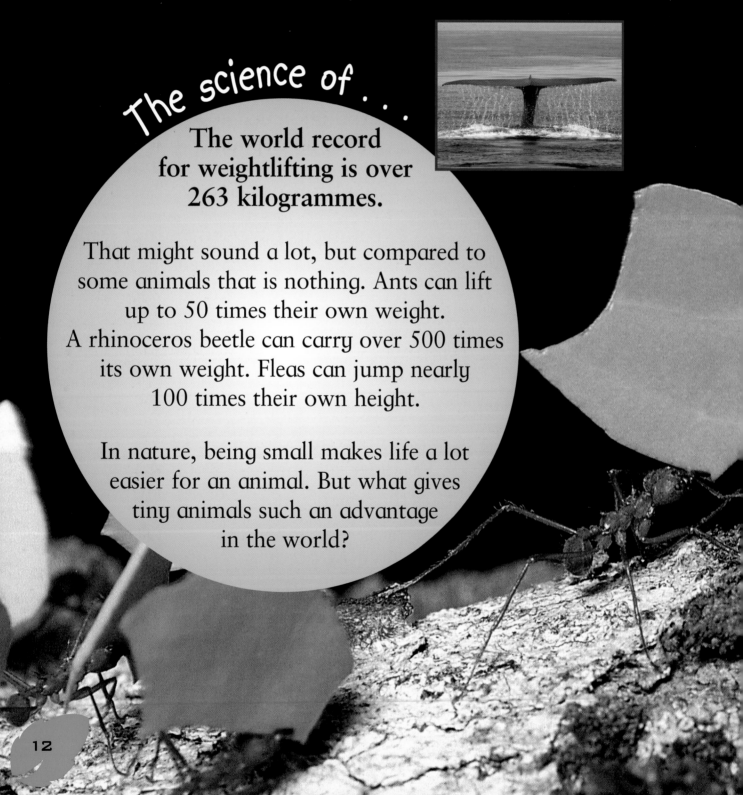

The science of . . .

The world record for weightlifting is over 263 kilogrammes.

That might sound a lot, but compared to some animals that is nothing. Ants can lift up to 50 times their own weight. A rhinoceros beetle can carry over 500 times its own weight. Fleas can jump nearly 100 times their own height.

In nature, being small makes life a lot easier for an animal. But what gives tiny animals such an advantage in the world?

How do we know?

There are many advantages to being a mini beast.
As animals get smaller, their strength relative to their environment increases enormously.

Because an elephant is so big and heavy, it could not jump without injuring itself. This is because the bones change in proportion to the animal's overall size. Even though the leg bones of an elephant are much bigger, they are not much stronger. The weight or length of a bone does not increase an animal's strength.

This means a flea, or even a mouse, can jump higher than an elephant.

A N ADULT SEA SQUIRT EATS ITS OWN BRAIN

Why do almost all animals have brains, but plants do not? Scientists believe it is because animals move around. They need a brain to tell their body what to do. To test this theory they looked at the sea squirt – an animal that doesn't move.

The science of . . .

YOUNG SEA SQUIRT

The sea squirt is a very unusual animal.

It starts off as a larva – a small creature like a tadpole. It has a head, a tail and, most importantly, a simple brain. When the larva finds a rock, it attaches itself to it and then grows into something that looks like a plant. Because it no longer moves, it no longer needs a brain. The brain slowly shrinks away.

Plants do not need to have a brain like animals, and yet the venus flytrap (*below*) can still catch flies!

How do we Know?

An animal needs to co-ordinate the different parts of its body in order to move.

Simple animals have just a few nerve cells to do this job. Higher animals have hundreds of millions of nerve cells. Nerve cells need to travel from the spinal cord to the end of the arms or legs. They need to tell the right part of the brain which muscle to move.

The human brain used to be about 20 per cent bigger than it is today. Although our brains are smaller, they are more complex with more connections. This means we don't need a large brain to be more intelligent.

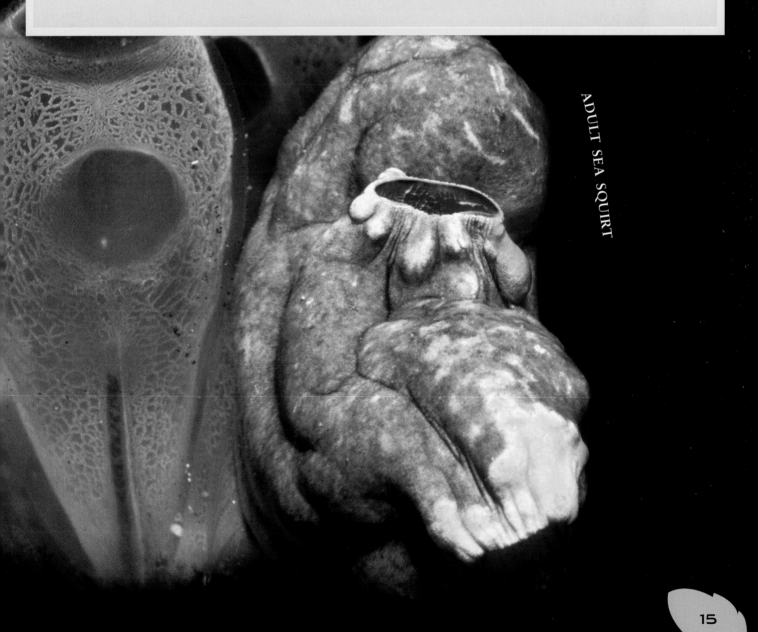

ADULT SEA SQUIRT

15

CRABS HAVE THEIR SKELETONS ON THE OUTSIDE

Humans have their skeleton on the inside to protect organs like the brain and the heart. Some species have it on the outside. This is called an exoskeleton.

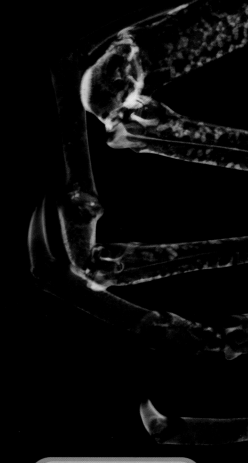

How do we know?

The animal kingdom is split into two halves – those with a skeleton (vertebrates) and those without (invertebrates).

Of the 10–20 million species alive on Earth, roughly 99 per cent are invertebrates.

Plants do not need a skeleton. They use water in their cells as support.

Crustacea (e.g. crabs) and insects do not have an internal skeleton like we do. They cover the outside of their bodies with a hard shell called an 'exoskeleton'.

The bones that make up your skeleton are all very much alive, growing and changing all the time like other parts of your body.

WOWZSAT!

The remains of animals' skeletons have been found in fossils. Because the soft parts rot away before the fossil forms, it is difficult to tell whether dinosaurs had fur, feathers or scales!

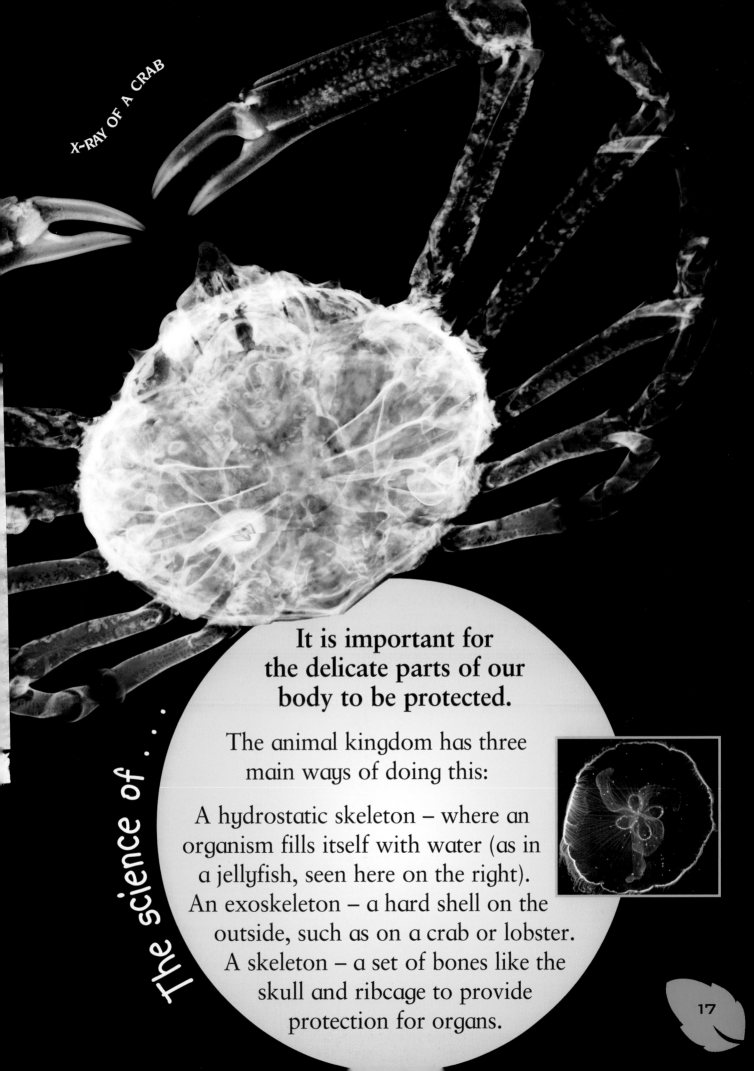

The science of ....

It is important for the delicate parts of our body to be protected.

The animal kingdom has three main ways of doing this:

A hydrostatic skeleton – where an organism fills itself with water (as in a jellyfish, seen here on the right). An exoskeleton – a hard shell on the outside, such as on a crab or lobster. A skeleton – a set of bones like the skull and ribcage to provide protection for organs.

17

How do we know?

All animals need to breathe in oxygen in order to stay alive.

Mammals, reptiles and birds have lungs that inhale oxygen and exhale carbon dioxide.

Insects and crustaceans do not have lungs. They have tiny tubes, called 'trachea', that allow air to get to different parts of the body. Trachea are not as efficient as lungs.

Mammals that live in water have to come to the surface to get oxygen. Fish and sharks do not have lungs. They have 'gills' that absorb oxygen as water flows through them.

Do sharks sleep? Scientists are not really sure. Because sharks never completely rest, they have to eat far more food than other fish of a similar size.

WOWZSAT!

Some sharks have learned how to take a rest. By wedging themselves in a cave, they can use the water current to flow over their gills and do all the hard work for them.

SHARKS HAVE TO KEEP SWIMMING IN ORDER TO STAY ALIVE

Sharks are among the oldest species alive on Earth today, and they are different to other fish.
Sharks are heavier than water. This means they have to keep swimming to stay alive.

The science of . . .

Sharks are heavy creatures. If they stop swimming they sink. If they stop moving completely, they drown!

Most fish have a special organ called a swim bladder. This is a small bag filled with air, which allows the fish to adjust its weight to the amount of water around it.

Mammals like whales and dolphins do not have swim bladders. Their lungs are full of air to help them float.

MONARCH BUTTERFLIES MIGRATE OVER GENERATIONS

Many animals spend their whole lives in one place. Others are forced to migrate every year in search of warmer weather. Monarch butterflies fly from Mexico to the United States and back every year.

The science of . . .

Monarch butterflies are the most remarkable migrators known in nature.

In spring, these butterflies fly north to the United States. Although they normally live for just one month, during migration they can stay alive for up to six months. They reproduce before they die, and generations later their offspring return to the same places as their parents. They are guided by their senses.

European eels also migrate, but their journey lasts a whole lifetime.

How do we know?

Many species migrate in large numbers. Scientists have tagged monarch butterflies and kept a record of their journeys.

Their records show that the butterflies travel over 1,500 kilometres.

Tagging has also been used to follow the migration of birds. Birds are usually tagged by putting a ring on their leg. Today, some animals, like salmon, are tagged by electronic transmitters. Large groups of birds can also be tracked with a type of radar that is usually used to track aeroplanes.

These detailed records are now starting to give us more details about the animals' migrating patterns. Some have changed quite dramatically. A change to the environment, caused by humans, is believed to be the main reason.

A FLYING EAGLE CAN SEE ITS PREY FROM OVER 5 KILOMETRES AWAY

Birds of prey have the most amazing eyesight. Other animals have specialised eyesight, too. Did you know that insects and snakes can see colours that mammals can't see? Or that octopuses' eyes are designed to produce a very clear image?

The science of . . .

Of all our senses, sight is probably the most useful and powerful.

There are three main types of eye in the animal world. Vertebrates have eyes very like our own. Insects have compound eyes that use many hundreds of very simple eyes together to produce an image. Cephalopods (e.g. octopus) also have eyes similar to ours.

Almost all animals have two eyes. This helps the brain judge distances. Birds of prey have the sharpest vision in the animal kingdom.

How do we know?

Eyes are a great advantage to any animal.

Vertebrate eyes suffer from one major drawback – the 'blind spot'. It lies where the optic nerve leads back into the brain. This means an object in the field of vision's blind spot is invisible.

One of the simplest eyes in nature is found in snakes. The Pit Viper gets its name from depressions (or pits) behind the nostrils that function as heat sensors. This means it is possible for the snake to locate warm-blooded prey even when it is dark.

WOWZSAT!

Birds of prey have over 100,000 light detecting cells per square mm on the back of each eye. That is more than ten times as many as humans have. This means birds of prey can see in fine detail.

How do we Know?

The reason a peacock can predict a storm is because of its sense of hearing.

Sound is a vibration in the air around us. Humans hear a limited pitch of sound – from about 20 to 20,000 waves per second; bats – 100,000 waves per second; peacocks and other birds – 0.2 waves per second. Storms emit very low-pitched sounds that can travel long distances which birds pick up.

Birds can also detect the magnetic field of the Earth, which helps homing pigeons and migrating birds find their way.

Did you know that many insects and birds are able to see colours far beyond the range of mammals?

PEACOCKS CAN PREDICT RAIN

Did you know that birds like peacocks can predict the coming of storms? Other animals react to natural disasters, such as earthquakes, long before humans are aware of the impending disaster. Biologists call these 'supersenses'.

The science of . . .

Mammals have five senses – touch, taste, hearing, smell and sight.

Many mammals have finer senses than humans. For instance, dogs are very good at picking up scents. Bats can locate a flying insect in complete darkness. Homing pigeons can find their way home from places they have never been in the dark.

Biologists are beginning to understand more by studying the senses and supersenses of the animal world.

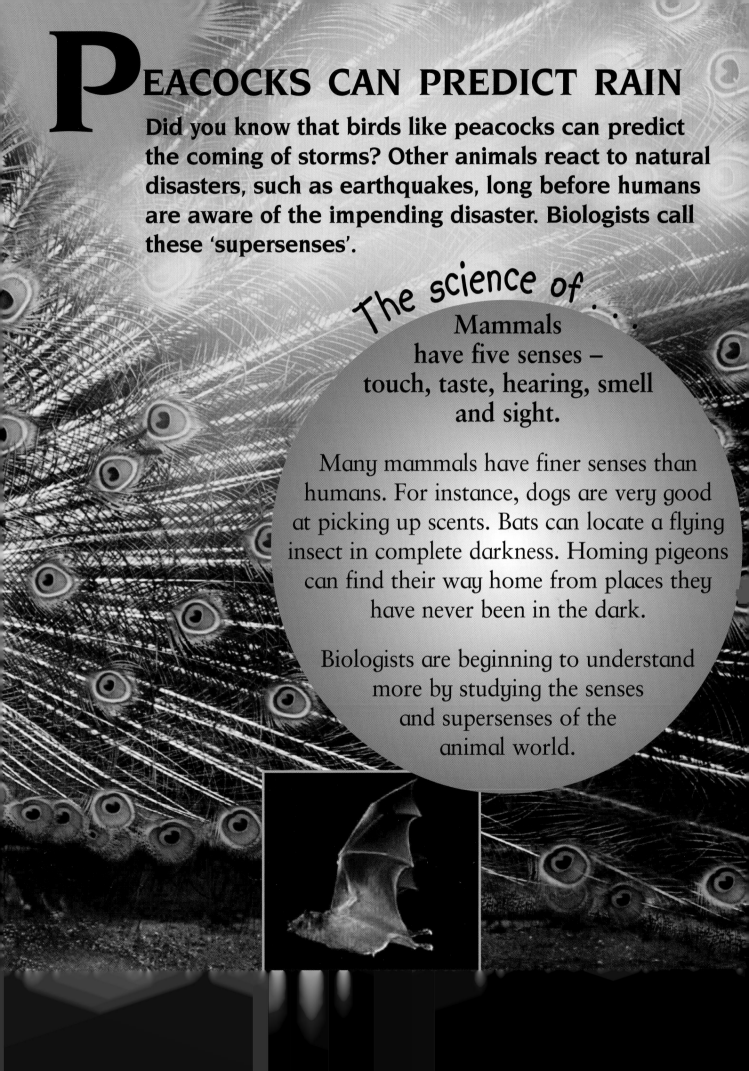

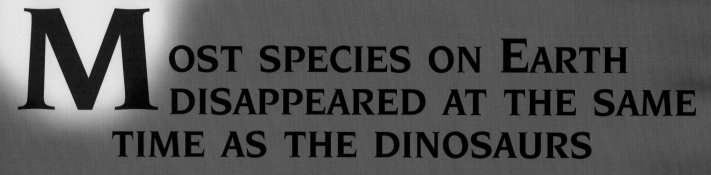

MOST SPECIES ON EARTH DISAPPEARED AT THE SAME TIME AS THE DINOSAURS

About 65 million years ago, every existing dinosaur species on Earth died out. So did many other plant and animal species both on land and in the sea.
So what happened?

The science of . . .

Dinosaurs were once the dominant species on Earth.

From the massive Brachiosaurus to the tiny Compsognathus, dinosaurs lived everywhere. However, 65 million years ago an event occurred which killed around 85 per cent of all living species.

All the animals alive today evolved from the species that survived. Scientists believe there have been several mass extinctions in the history of the Earth.

How do we know?

By studying fossils found in rocks, scientists believe they have found the answer.
At the time of the dinosaurs, it is thought that a meteorite or comet, 10 kilometres in diameter, collided with Earth. The energy it released was more powerful than 1,000 nuclear explosions.

The largest mass extinction occurred about 225 million years ago. Gases were released by the eruption of massive volcanoes, which led to global warming. Because of the high temperatures and reduction in oxygen, 90 per cent of marine life and over 70 per cent of land-based species died out.

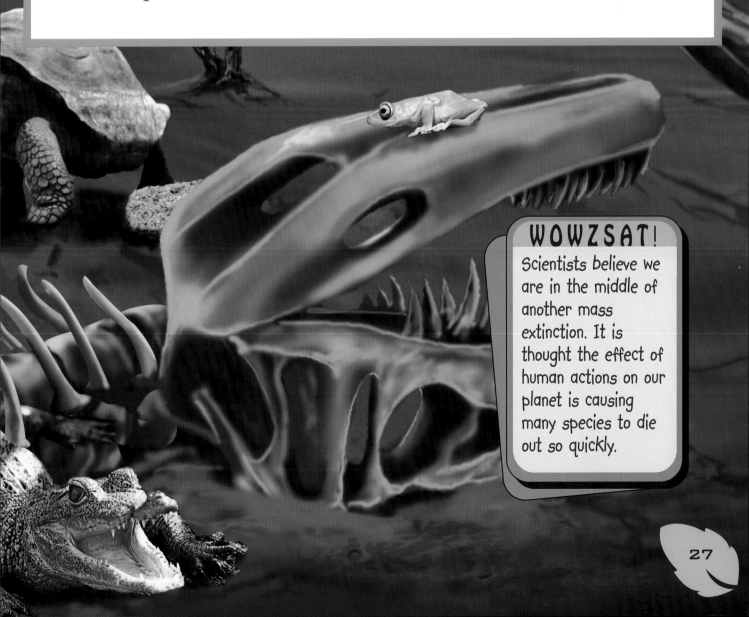

WOWZSAT!

Scientists believe we are in the middle of another mass extinction. It is thought the effect of human actions on our planet is causing many species to die out so quickly.

27

ANIMALS ADAPT TO LIVE AT OVER 100°C AND BELOW 0°C

Many animals have adapted to survive extreme temperatures. Some can even survive when their body temperature is colder than ice or hotter than boiling water.

The science of . . .

How can animals survive such extremes?

Tiny crustacea called krill live below the ice of the Arctic. They stay alive by using oils and fats to prevent the water in their bodies from freezing.

Some species of fish produce a molecule that is similar to the antifreeze we put in our car radiators. This means they can survive in conditions that would freeze other fish to death. Other creatures live deep down near vents in the ocean floor where the water temperature is over 120°C.

How do we Know?

Animals have learned to adapt to their environment over thousands of years.

Polar bears, for example, have adapted to the cold of the Arctic with a thick coat of fur and a layer of fat.

Lizards, and other animals who live in the desert, are wise enough to stay underground during the hottest and coldest parts of the day. Lizards have evolved long legs to help keep them cool from the hot desert sands.

Camels and desert rats have adapted to reabsorb vital water. In times of drought they have learnt how to turn their body fat into water. For species to adapt in the future, Earth must not change too quickly.

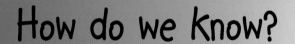

Glossary

Adaptation – Changing to suit the environment.

Cephalopod – A group of species including octopuses and cuttlefish.

Crustacea – A group of species including lobsters and crabs.

DNA (deoxyribonucleic acid) – a molecule that 'stores' the genetic code of living creatures.

Exoskeleton – An external skeleton found in many creatures.

Extinction – The death of every member of a species.

Fossil – The preserved remains of a dead animal.

Genetic code – The 'instructions' for how to produce the chemicals required for a living creature.

Gills – Organs used by many sea creatures to extract oxygen from the water.

Invertebrates – Animals that have no backbone.

Larva – The young form of some creatures.

Mammal – A group of species that feed their newborn infants milk.

Migrate – To move from one place to another due to the change of climate every year.

Organ – A part of a living creature that performs a specific function.

Senses – The methods by which a creature detects its surroundings.

Species – A group of animals that can all breed with each other.

Supersense – An animal sense that is better or different from the human senses.

Swim bladder – An organ that enables fish to adjust their buoyancy in water.

Trachea – A tube for transporting air within the body of a creature.

Vertebrates – Animals with a backbone.

Biography

Walter Alvarez (b. 1940) An American geologist who discovered iridium in rocks about 65 million years old.

Charles Darwin (1809-1882) An English biologist who proposed that natural selection led to evolutionary change.

Sir John Lubbock (1834-1913) An English biologist who studied the behaviour and senses of insects.

Gregor Mendel (1822-1884) An Austrian monk who taught both mathematics and biology.

Francis Crick (1916-2004), Rosalind Franklin (1920-1958), James Watson (b. 1928), and Maurice Wilkins (1916-2004). Four scientists who together worked out the shape and function of DNA. Crick and Watson worked out how DNA 'stored' and used the genetic code.

KEY DATES

500 BC – Xenophanes studies fossils.

350 BC – Aristotle classifies animal species in a series of books.

1680 – Anton van Leeuwenhoek sees bacteria with a microscope.

1859 – Charles Darwin publishes *Origin of Species*.

1865 – Gregor Mendel publishes his experiments on pea plants.

1952 – Franklin and Wilkins determine the general structure of DNA.

1953 – Crick and Watson determine the precise structure of DNA.

2001 – The human genetic code (genome) is determined by hundreds of collaborating scientists.

Index

Photocredits: l-left, r-right, b-bottom, t-top, c-centre, m-middle. Front cover c, 10-11 – Michael Mueller/Ingram Publishing/Q2A. Front cover bl, 5bm, 18-19 – Digital Stock. 1m, 16-17 – Photodisc. 2-3, 12-13, 12tr, 29, 31 – Digital Vision. 4bl, 24-25 – Digital Stock/Q2A. 4br, 6-7 – Q2A. 5t, 28 – Corbis. 5tm, 14-15 – RogerSteene/imagequestmarine.com/© Mary Lou Frost. 5m, 22-23 – Corbis/Q2A. 5b, 26-27 – Tony Waterer/Digital Vision/Q2A. 7br – Flick Smith. 8br, 9 – Ingram Publishing. 9bl – John Robinson. 10m – © Linda Gettmann. 14b – Michael Abrams. 17mr – NOAA Photo Library. 20-21, 30 – C F Gottfried/Monarcha A C. 22br – Corel. 25b – US Fish & Wildlife Service.